AIRCRAFT STRUCTURAL TECHNICIAN
Student Workbook

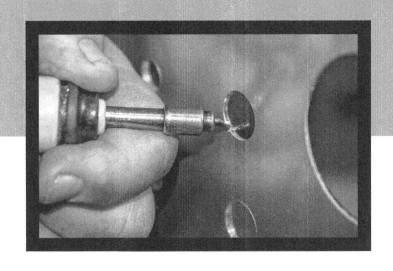

Production Staff

Designer/Photographer Dustin Blyer
Senior Designer/Production Manager Roberta Byerly
Editor Jeff Strong

International Standard Book Number 1-933189-11-8
ISBN 13: 978-1-933189-11-6
Order # T-AST-0102

For Sale by: Avotek
A Select Aerospace Industries, Inc., company

Mail to:
P.O. Box 219
Weyers Cave, VA 24486
USA

Ship to:
200 Packaging Drive
Weyers Cave, VA 24486
USA

Toll Free: 800-828-6835
Telephone: 540-234-9090
Fax: 540-234-9399

Third Printing
Printed in the USA

www.avotek.com

Contents

To the Student

This Student Workbook accompanies *Aircraft Structural Technician*. This workbook should be utilized as a tool for highlighting the strengths as well as pinpointing the weaknesses of the AMT student gathering the skill and knowledge necessary to build a strong foundation in the aircraft maintenance field. Specifically, it evaluates the progress made in applicable subject areas.

The foundation on which this workbook has been built assumes that the student is actively engaged in preparing for two goals: the first is to pass all required testing for the FAA Airframe and Powerplant Mechanic Certificate, and the second is to obtain the necessary skills and knowledge to function as an entry-level structural technician in the field. Both goals must be kept in mind and the material presented here has been designed to maintain that balance.

Each chapter of the text is divided into three question formats and printed on perforated sheets for removal and presentation. They are presented as follows:

Fill in the Blank

These questions are designed to help the student understand new terminology and fundamental facts essential to the understanding of section material.

Multiple Choice

These questions offer a broader overview of the material by offering several possible answers, and allowing the student to identify the correct answer either through recognition or through the process of elimination.

Analysis

These are complex questions that require the student to access information presented in the text, analyze the data, and record a response. Successful completion of the analysis questions shows the student has a thorough understanding of the material contained in the chapter.

The answers for each set of questions are available from your course instructor.

Email us at comments@avotek.com for comments or suggestions.

Avotek® Aircraft Maintenance Series

Introduction to Aircraft Maintenance

Aircraft Structural Maintenance

Aircraft System Maintenance

Aircraft Powerplant Maintenance

Avotek Aircraft Avionics Series

Avionics: Fundamentals of Aircraft Electronics

Avionics: Beyond the AET

Avionics: Instruments and Auxiliary Systems

Avionics: Systems and Troubleshooting

Other Books by Avotek

Advanced Composites

Aircraft Corrosion Control Guide

Aircraft Hydraulics

Aircraft Structural Technician

Aircraft Turbine Engines

Aircraft Wiring & Electrical Installation

AMT Reference Handbook

Avotek Aeronautical Dictionary

Fundamentals of Modern Aviation

Light Sport Aircraft Inspection Procedures

Structural Composites: Advanced Composites in Aviation

Transport Category Aircraft Systems

1. A _____ is an aircraft with an upper and lower set of wings.

2. The five main units of the airframe of a fixed-wing aircraft are: the fuselage, wings, stabilizers, flight control surfaces, and _____ .

3. _____ is always the principal requirement in aircraft structures, even those parts that are not necessarily primary structures.

4. _____ is the ability of the metal in an aircraft to withstand being pulled apart.

5. The motion caused when one end of an object is twisted one way and the other end is twisted the opposite way is called _____ .

6. The superstructure that houses all the parts necessary to make an aircraft fly is called the _____ .

7. In a _____ fuselage, the skin of the aircraft carries the primary structural load of the fuselage.

8. _____ are numbered in inches from a reference point knows as the reference datum.

9. There are two types of wing design used in modern aircraft: _____ and _____ .

10. A _____ is used to prevent vibrations in a long strut during flight.

11. Drag and anti-drag wires are often called _____ . These wires are used to square and give rigidity to each wing bay.

12. Wing station 0 (zero) is located at the center line of the _____ , and all wing stations are measured outward from that point in inches.

13. A _____ type of wing construction uses two main longitudinal members with connecting bulkheads.

14. The _____ is the primary load carrying member running parallel to the lateral axis of each wing of an aircraft.

15. Former ribs are not considered primary structure, but _____ are main structural wing parts.

16. A nacelle contains a _____ that separates the engine compartment from the area aft of the engine.

Chapter 1
Aircraft Structures

FILL IN THE BLANK QUESTIONS

name:

date:

Chapter 1
Aircraft Structures

FILL IN THE BLANK QUESTIONS

name:

date:

17. Engine _____ is a set of detachable, permanently formed skins designed to streamline the airflow around an engine and to provide cooling.

18. A _____ is a horizontal stabilizer that moves instead of an elevator to raise and lower the aircraft's nose.

19. The rudder moves the aircraft about the _____ axis.

20. The _____ move the aircraft about the longitudinal axis.

21. The elevators move the aircraft about the _____ axis.

22. If the left aileron is moved down, the right aileron moves _____ .

23. Wing _____ given an aircraft extra lift.

24. _____ are auxiliary wing flight control surfaces mounted on the upper surface of each wing that operate with the ailerons to provide lateral control.

25. _____ smooth the airflow over the angles formed by the junction of the wing with the fuselage.

1. Which one of these is not a principal unit of the airframe of a fixed-wing aircraft?
   a. Fuselage
   b. Stabilizers
   c. Flight control surfaces
   d. Cowling

2. The five major stresses to which all aircraft are subjected are tension, compression, torsion, shear, and:
   a. Regression
   b. Extension
   c. Bending
   d. Breaking

3. Strength that resists the stress of a crushing force is called:
   a. Compression
   b. Bending
   c. Kryptonia
   d. Shear

4. Which type of fuselage is constructed of chrome-molybedenum steel tubing welded together?
   a. Monocoque type
   b. Truss type
   c. Semi-monocoque type
   d. Tubular type

5. In a semi-monocoque fuselage, heavy one-piece parts made from heat-treated aluminum alloys that are extruded or formed are called:
   a. Stringers
   b. Longerons
   c. Splice joints
   d. Gussets

6. Connecting brackets that hold stringers to former rings are called:
   a. Bulkheads
   b. Longerons
   c. Splice joints
   d. Gussets

7. In the location numbering system used on most large aircraft, the tip of the nose cone is station:
   a. X
   b. Zero
   c. Ten
   d. Six

8. What is the term for a width measurement left or right of, and parallel to, the vertical center line of an aircraft?
   a. Water line
   b. Goal line
   c. Buttock or butt line
   d. Aileron line

9. What type of wing is built so that no external bracing is needed?
   a. Semi-cantilever
   b. Full cantilever
   c. Bi-wing
   d. Left wing

Chapter 1
Aircraft Structures

10. Which of these is not a fundamental type of wing design?
    a. Monospar
    b. Box beam
    c. Tapered edge
    d. Multi-spar

11. Which type of wing design incorporates more than one main longitudinal member in its construction?
    a. Monospar
    b. Box beam
    c. Tapered edge
    d. Multi-spar

12. Structural crosspieces in an aircraft wing that begin at the leading edge and shape the contour of the wing to its trailing edge are called:
    a. Spars
    b. Ribs
    c. Wing butts
    d. Outer skin

13. A wing that stores fuel without the use of a conventional fuel tank is called a:
    a. Wet wing
    b. West wing
    c. Fuel wing
    d. Octane enhancement wing

14. Streamlined enclosures used on multi-engine aircraft to house engines or landing gear are called pods or:
    a. Honeycomb ribs
    b. Monocoques
    c. Wheel wells
    d. Nacelles

15. A set of permanently formed skins that fit over an engine and help to cool the engine is called:
    a. Jet streaming
    b. Cowling
    c. Nacelles
    d. Wing pylons

16. The cowling on most large jet transports is designed to provide high by-pass of air between the cowling and the:
    a. Wing pylons
    b. Outer engine
    c. Engine core
    d. Firewall

17. The tail section of a fixed-wing aircraft is called the:
    a. Empennage
    b. Stabilators
    c. Water line
    d. Elevators

18. Which of these is not a major axis of an aircraft?
    a. Actuating
    b. Vertical
    c. Longitudinal
    d. Lateral

19. A dive brake is considered which type of flight control?
    a. Primary
    b. Secondary
    c. Tertiary
    d. Auxiliary

20. Control surfaces on an aircraft are primarily made of aluminum alloy or
    a. Rubberized materials
    b. Advanced composites
    c. Steel
    d. Sealant and protective finish

21. What is the term for a control surface on a V-tail aircraft that combines the function of the standard rudder and elevators?
    a. Aileron
    b. Elerudder
    c. Ruddervator
    d. None of the above

22. After moveable controls are repaired, they also need to be:
    a. Rebalanced
    b. Restabilized
    c. Restrained
    d. Recentered

23. Aircraft requiring extra wing area to help with lift often use:
    a. Plain split flaps
    b. Leading edge flags
    c. Kruger-type flags
    d. Fowler flaps

24. What type of flap uses magnesium casting as its principal structural component?
    a. Plain split flaps
    b. Leading edge flags
    c. Kruger-type flags
    d. Fowler flaps

25. What type of flap is designed to be used when descending at a steep angle?
    a. Fowler flaps
    b. Spoilers
    c. Wing fairings
    d. Speed brakes

26. The outer covering of an aircraft is called the:
    a. Fuselage
    b. Structural member
    c. Skin
    d. Surface

Chapter 1
Aircraft Structures

MULTIPLE CHOICE
QUESTIONS

name:

date:

1. Name the primary consideration in the design of aircraft structures. What other properties of the structure must also be considered?

2. Why does an aircraft technician have to understand the stresses that can act on an aircraft? After all, the technician doesn't have to design the aircraft.

ANALYSIS QUESTIONS

name:

date:

3. Name and define the five main types of stress that act on an aircraft and give an example of each.

4. There are three main types of fuselage construction. Name them and give their characteristics.

5. How does an aircraft designer or manufacturer describe the location of various parts of the aircraft? What are some of the reference points in an aircraft diagram?

6. There are two main types of wing design. What are they, and what makes each one different from the other?

7. How do wing spars, ribs, and stringers work to provide structural strength to an aircraft wing?

8. Describe the components of an engine nacelle or pod and the function of each component.

9. What are the three axes of an aircraft, and what sets of flight control surfaces move the aircraft in relation to each of its axes?

10. Describe the purpose of wing flaps.

1. *Ferrous* refers to a group of metals that have _____ as their principal constituent.

2. The ability of a material to resist stress without breaking is known as _____ .

3. The _____ is a measure of the relationship between the strength of a material and its weight per cubic inch.

4. A metal that can be easily hammered or rolled into various shapes without cracking or breaking is said to be _____ .

5. _____ is the ability of a metal to become liquid by the application of heat.

FILL IN THE BLANK QUESTIONS

name:

date:

6. Commercially pure aluminum has a tensile strength of _____ p.s.i., but through various alloying processes, the tensile strength can be raised to _____ p.s.i., similar to structural steel.

7. Aluminum alloy in the 3000 series is aluminum combined with _____ .

8. The _____ digit in an aluminum alloy designation indicates alloy modifications.

9. The _____ process for aluminum alloys involves heating the metal, holding the metal at that temperature for a given period of time, and then cooling the metal in still air.

10. The time that a metal must be kept at a specified temperature, starting at the time the coldest part of the metal reaches the minimum limit of the temperature range, is called _____ .

11. Large forgings and heavy sections of metal are usually quenched using the _____ quenching method.

12. To prevent or greatly reduce the possibility of corrosion in aluminum/copper and aluminum/zinc alloys, a process called _____ heat treatment is used.

13. Strength, hardness, and elasticity are increased by strain hardening, but _____ decreases.

14. Under normal conditions, pure _____ almost never corrodes.

15. _____ is the world's lightest structural metal.

16. If carbon is added to iron, the resulting metal is called _____ .

17. The principal alloy of stainless steel is _____ .

Chapter 2
Metals

18. The process of _____ removes the internal stresses caused by welding, machining, or forming steel.

19. _____ reduces the brittleness of steel and also softens it. It involves heating the steel to below the critical temperature, holding the metal at that temperature for at least an hour, and then cooling it in the air.

20. _____ is a casehardening process in which carbon is added to the surface of low-carbon steel.

21. Casehardening steel with the use of ammonia gas is called _____ .

22. The _____ is determined by measuring the diameter of the impression left on a piece of metal by a hardened ball.

23. The _____ is the ratio of the load applied to the surface area of the indentation left on a piece of metal by a small diamond.

24. Microhardness testing can be performed with either a _____ or Vickers indenter.

25. Some heat-treated aluminum alloys containing several percent of _____ will turn black after the sample is immersed in a solution of caustic soda.

1. The point at which a load would cause an initial indication of a permanent distortion is called:
   a. Tensile strength
   b. Yield strength
   c. Shear strength
   d. Bearing strength

2. What type of strength is measured by the resistance of a material to a force that would tend to pull it apart?
   a. Tensile strength
   b. Yield strength
   c. Shear strength
   d. Bearing strength

3. If a bolt were installed in a hole that was too large, and the head was pulled through the material when torque was applied, it means that what measure of strength of the material was insufficient?
   a. Tensile strength
   b. Yield strength
   c. Shear strength
   d. Bearing strength

4. The ability of a metal to resist abrasion, penetration, cutting action, or permanent distortion is called what?
   a. Hardness
   b. Malleability
   c. Ductility
   d. Toughness

5. Metal that allows for little bending or forming without shattering is called what?
   a. Hard
   b. Conductive
   c. Brittle
   d. Nonferrous

6. This property of metal enables it to return to its natural shape.
   a. Brittleness
   b. Elasticity
   c. Ferrousity
   d. Fusibility

7. Aluminum alloys become liquid at approximately what temperature?
   a. 2,600°F
   b. 2,000°F
   c. 1,250°F
   d. 98.6°F

8. Which of these is not a property of aluminum that makes it advantageous in modern aircraft construction?
   a. High strength-to-weight ratio
   b. Excellent conductivity
   c. Melts at a relatively low temperature
   d. Contains steel

9. Which of these thickness measurements is outside of the normal range for aluminum alloys used in small aircraft construction?
   a. 0.025″
   b. 0.166″
   c. 0.075″
   d. 0.086″

Chapter 2
Metals

MULTIPLE CHOICE
QUESTIONS

name:

date:

10. An aluminum/silicon alloy is denoted by which series number?
    a. 4000
    b. 6000
    c. 2000
    d. 9000

11. Which of these is not a standard method of quenching heated metal?
    a. Cold-water quenching
    b. Oil-based quenching
    c. Hot-water quenching
    d. Spray quenching

12. Which of these temper designations indicates "strain hardened and partially annealed"?
    a. -F
    b. -O
    c. -@
    d. -H2

13. Which of these temper designations indicates "solution heat treated and then artificially aged"?
    a. -T4
    b. -T5
    c. -T6
    d. -T12

14. If an aluminum alloy sheet has undergone cladding with pure aluminum, and its thickness is 0.050", how thick is the cladding on each side?
    a. 0.0050"
    b. 0.0025"
    c. 0.0250"
    d. 0.0500"

15. Which of these items should you keep in mind when choosing substitute metal for use in aircraft repair?
    a. Maintaining the original strength of the structure
    b. Maintaining the original weight
    c. Maintaining contour or aerodynamic properties
    d. All of these

16. Which of the following is not a metal commonly alloyed with magnesium?
    a. Aluminum
    b. Silver
    c. Manganese
    d. Zinc

17. Which of these is a nickel alloy?
    a. Monel
    b. Alpha alloy
    c. Carbon steel
    d. Vanadium

18. Nickel steels are primarily used in which aircraft parts?
    a. Landing gear
    b. Structural members
    c. Hardware, like nuts and bolts
    d. Engine nacelles

19. Generally speaking, which of these is an advantage of ferrous metals over nonferrous metals?
    a. Only ferrous metals can be annealed
    b. Only ferrous metals can be normalized
    c. Only ferrous metals can be formed
    d. Only ferrous metals can be hardened by heat treatment

20. When hardening carbon steel, it must be cooled to below 1,000°F within what time limit?
    a. Less than 1 second
    b. Less than 10 seconds
    c. Within a minute
    d. Before sunrise

21. Which of these is not a common method of carburizing steel?
    a. Liquid carburizing
    b. Instant carburizing
    c. Gas carburizing
    d. Pack carburizing

22. One method of testing the hardness of metals involves measuring the depth of penetration of a diamond cone or a hardened steel ball under pressure into the metal. It is called the:
    a. Brinell Hardness Testing System
    b. Microhardness testing
    c. Vickers Hardness Test
    d. Rockwell Hardness Testing System

23. To measure the hardness of precision work pieces that are too small to be measured by other tests, you could use:
    a. Brinell Hardness Testing System
    b. Microhardness testing
    c. Webster Hardness Gauge
    d. Rockwell Hardness Testing System

24. Which hardness testing system looks like a set of pliers with a dial attached?
    a. Brinell Hardness Testing System
    b. Microhardness testing
    c. Webster Hardness Gauge
    d. Rockwell Hardness Testing System

25. Quantitative inspection of metals includes:
    a. Chemical composition
    b. Mechanical properties
    c. Dimensional requirement
    d. All of these

Chapter 2
Metals

MULTIPLE CHOICE
QUESTIONS

name:

date:

1. What makes knowledge of metal and its properties so important to aircraft maintenance technicians?

ANALYSIS
QUESTIONS

name:

date:

2. How can the hardness of a metal be increased?

3. There are two types of conductivity. What are they, and what considerations come into play for each of them when working on an aircraft?

4. Why is the density of a metal important in choosing material to be used in aircraft?

5. What does each of the four digits in the index numbering system used with aluminum alloys indicate?

6. Describe the process of heat treating aluminum alloys. How is it different from heat treating ferrous metals?

7. What can be dangerous about large sections of magnesium alloys? How about magnesium dust or fine chips?

8. Describe the tempering process for steel.

9. Describe three methods of carburizing steel. What effect does carburizing have?

10. If you examine the edge of a clad aluminum alloy with a magnifying glass, what will you see?

1. Hammers and mallets are used to drive other tools or to _____ metal.

2. A _____ hammer is used to smooth the surface of parts that have already been formed.

3. Various types of _____ are used to install grommets and fasteners, to make holes, or transfer locations from patterns to sheet metal.

4. The 6-inch _____ pliers is the preferred size for use in repair work.

5. A _____ is a hard steel tool that can be used for cutting and chipping any metal softer than the tool itself.

6. The _____ is never included in the length of a file.

7. Dutchmen snips are also known as _____ snips.

8. The most common types of wood saws are the _____ and rip saws.

9. The _____ of a hacksaw blade indicates the number of teeth per inch.

10. A _____ drill motor is recommended around flammable material.

11. The two types of auger drill bits are the _____ and solid center.

12. A _____ is a pointed tool that is rotated to cut holes in material.

13. The most desirable drill bit for aluminum alloy sheet metal has an _____ of 135° and a split point.

14. A _____ countersink is adjustable to any depth, and its cutters are interchangeable.

15. A common screwdriver must fill at least _____ percent of the screw slot. Otherwise, it cuts and burrs the slot, making it worthless.

16. A _____ screwdriver has a six-pointed blade.

17. A _____ is used to remove nuts and bolts that resist other means of removal.

18. When a definite, measured pressure must be applied to a nut or bolt, you should use a _____ wrench.

19. _____ calipers should not be used for precision measurement.

20. A scriber is used to mark lines on _____ surfaces.

FILL IN THE BLANK QUESTIONS

name:

date:

FILL IN THE BLANK
QUESTIONS

name:

date:

21. Sheet metal is often formed or finished over anvils known as _____ and stakes.

22. Hardwood _____ are widely used in airframe metalwork for shrinking or stretching metal, especially angles and flanges.

23. A holding device attached to a workbench is called a _____ .

24. A Rotex _____ has two cylindrical turrets containing dies and punches, one above the other, that are rotated to select holes of an indicated diameter.

25. To punch a keyed hole for an electrical switch, use a _____ punch.

26. For drilling holes in sheet metal with a hand-held drill, an air powered motor is preferred. But when you are using a drill as a powered screwdriver, a _____ motor is indispensable.

27. A machine with an abrasive wheel that removes excess material while producing a suitable surface is generally known as a _____ .

28. The _____ of a brake or folder indicates the gauge and size of metal that can be bent using the tool.

29. Shrinking and stretching machines are designed for use with metal that has been _____ .

30. A _____ works by pressing the material to be formed around a die using a rubber blanket to apply pressure.

1. What type of hammer has a rounded head and is used for forming soft metal or flattening rivet heads?
   a. Rawhide faced
   b. Ball-peen
   c. Carpenter's
   d. Sledge

2. What type of mallet face should you use on copper?
   a. Soft
   b. Medium
   c. Tough
   d. Extra hard

3. This type of punch is used to create an indentation in metal in order to hold the point of a drill when starting a hole.
   a. Prick
   b. Center
   c. Roundhouse
   d. Starting

4. Which of these is a type of slip-joint pliers with the jaws set at an angle to the handles, and is used to grasp packing nuts, pipe, or odd-shaped parts?
   a. Self-locking
   b. Needlenose
   c. Water pump
   d. Duckbill

5. Which of these is not a distinguishing characteristic of a file?
   a. Coarseness of the teeth
   b. Grip
   c. Length
   d. Cut

6. Aviation snips have color-coded handles to indicate what type of cutting they are for. What are green handled snips used for?
   a. Straight cutting
   b. Saw cutting
   c. Cutting left
   d. Cutting right

7. A rip saw is used to cut:
   a. With the grain
   b. Against the grain
   c. Where no grain exists
   d. Metal

8. Which type of drill bit is used to cut shallow, flat-bottomed holes?
   a. Jennings
   b. Forstner
   c. Spade
   d. Any strong bit will work

9. The standard commercial drill is called:
   a. Aircraft extension
   b. Taper length
   c. Jobber length
   d. Stub screw

10. The most common material used to fabricate drills is:
    a. Carbon steel
    b. High-speed steel (HSS)
    c. Carbide
    d. Cobalt

MULTIPLE CHOICE QUESTIONS

name:

date:

name:

date:

Chapter 3
Hand Tools and Measuring Devices

MULTIPLE CHOICE QUESTIONS

11. Which tool, used to cut larger-diameter holes in sheet metal, has an adjustable radius?
    a. Circular hole cutter
    b. Countersink
    c. Fly cutter
    d. Reamer

12. A tool that cuts a cone-shaped depression around a hole in order to allow a rivet to set flush with the surface of the material is called a:
    a. Countersink
    b. Kitchen sink
    c. Reamer
    d. Fly cutter

13. Which tool is used to cut threads on the inside of a hole?
    a. Screwdriver
    b. Taper
    c. Tap
    d. Die

14. Which tool is used to cut external threads on round stock?
    a. Screwdriver
    b. Taper
    c. Tap
    d. Die

15. Which kind of wrench comprises a round metal sleeve with a square drive opening that attaches to a handle and a 6- or 12-point opening on the other end to fit a nut or bolt?
    a. Socket
    b. Combination
    c. Box-end
    d. Monkey

16. Rules, calipers, and scribers are examples of what kind of tool?
    a. Wrench tools
    b. Measuring and layout tools
    c. Pounding tools
    d. Cutting tools

17. Which of these tasks is not performed using a divider or calipers?
    a. Scribe a circle
    b. Draw an arc
    c. Attach fasteners
    d. Transfer a measurement from a rule to the work

18. Some micrometers have a feature that allows you to read directly the fraction of a division that is indicated on the thimble scale. This feature is called a:
    a. Caliper
    b. Combination set
    c. Vernier scale
    d. Barrel scale

19. The most commonly used sheet-metal holder is:
    a. Cleco fastner
    b. C-Clamp
    c. Metal screw
    d. Magnet

20. Which popular shop tool cuts metal with an upper blade controlled by a foot treadle?
    a. Cleco fastener
    b. Squaring shear
    c. Chassis punch
    d. Snips

21. Which of these metal-cutting powered tools has a circular cutting blade and can be useful for removing the damaged portions of a stringer?
    a. Saber saw
    b. Nibbler
    c. Drill press
    d. Panel saw

22. Which of these metal-cutting power tools uses a high-speed blanking action to cut out pieces of metal up to about $1/16$ of an inch wide?
    a. Saber saw
    b. Nibbler
    c. Drill press
    d. Panel saw

23. To drill holes that require a high degree of accuracy, use:
    a. An air powered hand drill
    b. A battery powered hand drill
    c. A drill press
    d. A hole deburring tool such as a countersink

24. Which of these is a hazard associated with the use of a grinder?
    a. A loose abrasive wheel
    b. A loose tool rest
    c. Not wearing eye protection
    d. All of these

25. Which tool would you use to form a small hem along the edge of a piece of sheet metal?
    a. Bar folder
    b. Nibbler
    c. Press brake
    d. Slip roll former

26. If you are using a cornice brake to form a 90° angle, what to what angle should you set the brake to in order to account for metal springback?
    a. 87°
    b. 90°
    c. 93°
    d. There is no setting required—just bend the metal and measure the angle

27. This metal forming tool can be used to form all four sides of a junction box from a single piece.
    a. Bar folder
    b. Box and pan break
    c. Cornice brake
    d. Slip roll former

28. To form a curved piece of sheet metal, use:
    a. Bar folder
    b. Box and pan break
    c. Cornice brake
    d. Slip roll former

29. One expensive machine used to fabricate replacement wing ribs or bulkheads, for example, very accurately and requiring little if any hand forming or straightening is:
    a. A flange former
    b. A slip roll former
    c. An English wheel
    d. A foot-operated stretcher

30. Which of these machines has an upper and lower roller between which sheet metal is pushed back and forth in order to form a compound curve?
    a. Flange former
    b. Slip roll former
    c. English wheel
    d. Foot-operated stretcher

1. Describe the safety considerations and techniques for using pounding tools.

2. Explain the difference between crossfiling and drawfiling.

ANALYSIS
QUESTIONS

name:

date:

3. Explain how to use a tin snips to cut sheet metal. How is it different from a hacksaw?

4. Different types of metal require different types of hacksaw blades. What term is used to indicate different kinds of blades, and what blades should you use for various types of metal?

5. What must you do before drilling a hole in hard material if you are using a drill bit with an included angle of 135° or more? Why?

6. Explain the difference between, and the uses of, the three types of taps in a set for a given diameter and thread series.

7. You are using an angle extension on a torque wrench (like the one in Figure 3-15-2B). The wrench itself is 10 inches long, and the extension is 4 inches long. What torque wrench reading should you reach if you want to apply 100 actual inch-pounds of torque?

8. Describe the parts of a combination set and their uses.

9. Describe how to read the measure on the barrel, thimble, and vernier scales in the lower left-hand picture in Figure 3-16-5.

10. Describe the process for squaring a sheet of metal with a squaring shears.

11. How can you drill a hole in a tight place where a straight drill motor just doesn't fit?

12. Describe a grinding wheel, what they are made out of, and how their abrasive quality is indicated. What material can be worked with each type of wheel?

ANALYSIS
QUESTIONS

name:

date:

1. A medium-sized transport plane requires more than _____ rivets.

2. The letters MS in a rivet classification code stands for _____ .

3. In the rivet classification code MS20426 D-5-8, the 5 indicates the _____ of the rivet in thirty-seconds of an inch.

4. A(n) _____ type rivet is fabricated from aluminum alloy 2117.

5. A(n) _____ type rivet is fabricated from aluminum alloy 2024.

6. Selecting a rivet made of the proper aluminum alloy is important because rivets carry _____ stress.

7. It is generally a bad idea to drive a _____ rivet into soft metal.

8. Use a rivet whose diameter is _____ times the thickness of the thickest section through which the rivet is driven, to the next larger $1/32$ of an inch.

9. The correct length of a rivet equals the sum of the thickness of the metal plus _____ times the diameter of the rivet shank.

10. The height of a rivet's bucktail should be _____ the diameter of the rivet.

11. The width of a rivet's bucktail should be at least _____ times the rivet diameter.

12. To do hand riveting, you need two tools: a hammer and a _____ .

13. If the hole for a rivet is too small and the rivet has to be forced into it, tiny grooves may be left on the _____ of the rivet, affecting its strength.

14. Most riveting is done with a _____ riveter.

15. For _____ riveting, use a rivet set with a flat or slightly crowned face.

16. When you rivet with a pneumatic riveter, work with a partner. One of you will operate the riveter while the other holds _____ against the rivet shank on the opposite side of the parts to be riveted.

17. A _____ crack by a flush rivet hole can be caused by a bad hole or a dimple that is too deep.

18. _____ cracking is normally caused by performing the dimpling operation at too low a temperature.

19. The outer rim of a countersunk rivet is between 0.004 and _____ inches thick, depending on the rivet diameter.

20. One of the types of sets used to drive flush rivets, known as a _____ is made in one piece.

21. After countersunk rivets have been set, you can use a rivet _____ to ensure that the surface is flush and smooth.

22. The _____ was an engineering group formed by the predecessor to the FAA in the early 1930s.

23. To create a leakproof seal in an integral fuel tank, the _____ head of the rivet is generally placed on the fuel side of the structure because it swells the most during driving.

24. Rivets can be heat treated in two ways: in a bath of _____ or in a hot air furnace.

25. The single shear strength of a 2117-T rivet with a diameter of $5/32$ of an inch is _____ .

1. Which type of rivet is the current standard and may be used to replace any raised-head rivet?
   a. Brazier Head
   b. Flat head
   c. Countersunk
   d. Universal head

2. Which type of rivet offers the least resistance to airflow?
   a. Brazier Head
   b. Flat head
   c. Countersunk
   d. Universal head

3. Which type of rivet is identified by a raised cross on the head?
   a. 5056-T, type B
   b. 2017-T, type D
   c. 2117-T, type AD
   d. 2024-T, type DD

4. Which type of rivet is identified by a dimple in the center of its the head?
   a. 5056-T, type B
   b. 2017-T, type D
   c. 2117-T, type AD
   d. 2024-T, type DD

5. Which type of rivet is identified by two raised bars on opposite sides of its the head?
   a. 5056-T, type B
   b. 2017-T, type D
   c. 2117-T, type AD
   d. 2024-T, type DD

6. Which of these things should you consider when choosing a rivet for a particular task?
   a. Rivet composition
   b. Rivet diameter
   c. Rivet length
   d. All of these

7. If a rivet will go through two sheets of metal, one of which is $1/16$ of an inch thick and the other of which is $1/32$ of an inch thick, what diameter rivet should you select?
   a. $1/16$
   b. $3/32$
   c. $5/32$
   d. $3/16$

8. If a rivet passes through two sheets of metal, each $1/16$ of an inch thick, and has a shank of $1/4$ inch, what length should the rivet be?
   a. $1/4$ inch
   b. $3/8$ inch
   c. $1/2$ inch
   d. As long as possible

9. Rivets should be spaced not less than a distance of three times the rivet diameter and not more than:
   a. 12 times the diameter
   b. 10 times the diameter
   c. 6 times the diameter
   d. 4 times the diameter

Chapter 4
Aircraft Riveting

MULTIPLE CHOICE QUESTIONS

name:

date:

10. Rivets should be spaced in from the edge of the sheet an absolute minimum of:
    a. Four times the rivet diameter
    b. Three times the rivet diameter
    c. Two times the rivet diameter
    d. The rivet diameter

11. Which aluminum alloy is used to make rivets that are the most widely used for aircraft structural parts?
    a. 2117-T
    b. 2017-T
    c. 2020-T
    d. 2024-T

12. Which aluminum alloy is used to make rivets that are used almost exclusively in highly stressed fittings?
    a. 2117-T
    b. 2017-T
    c. 2020-T
    d. 2024-T

13. Which of these is not one of the three most common aluminum alloys used to make rivets used in aircraft construction and repair?
    a. 2117-T
    b. 2017-T
    c. 2020-T
    d. 2024-T

14. A marred rivet head after the rivet has been bucked was caused by using a set one size too small, or:
    a. A crooked bucking bar
    b. Not centering the set on the rivet head
    c. Covering only part of the shank with the bucking bar
    d. Using the wrong aluminum alloy in the rivet

15. A "smile" or "eyebrow" next to a rivet that has been driven is usually caused by:
    a. Insufficient air pressure on the hammer
    b. Holding the set at an angle and allowing it to contact the sheet
    c. Holding the bucking bar at an angle
    d. Not centering the set on the rivet

16. In flush riveting, pressing the metal around a rivet hole to the proper shape using a die is called:
    a. Countersinking
    b. Radius dimpling
    c. Cut countersinking
    d. Coin dimpling

17. The standard rivet for flush riveting is the:
    a. 90-degree rivet
    b. Dimpling die rivet
    c. 100-degree countersunk rivet
    d. AN125 78-degree rivet

18. When the lower sheet of metal to be flush riveted is thicker, you could dimple the upper sheet and do what to the lower sheet?
    a. Cut-countersink it
    b. Radium dimple it
    c. Nothing—the dimple in the upper sheet will take care of the lower sheet too
    d. Use a draw set

19. NACA riveting refers to countersinking:
    a. Every other rivet
    b. The shop head of a rivet rather than the manufactured head
    c. The manufactured head of a rivet rather than the shop head
    d. Using a repair washer

20. The most common liquid used in wet riveting is:
    a. Chromium paste
    b. Molten aluminum
    c. Zinc oxide primer
    d. Zinc chromate primer

21. In the rivet type identifier 2117-T, the "T" indicates:
    a. The manufacturer
    b. That the rivet was heat-treated
    c. That the rivet was not heat-treated
    d. Nothing

22. Which two types of rivets can be used without being heat-treated?
    a. A and D
    b. A and DD
    c. D and DD
    d. A and AD

23. When treating 2017 rivets in a hot air furnace, the rivets should be soaked at a temperature of:
    a. 925° to 950°F
    b. 910° to 930°F
    c. About 800°F
    d. 910° to 960°F

24. Rivets must be quenched within how long of removing them from the heat-treating furnace or they will lose the qualities that heat-treating provides.
    a. 1 minute
    b. 20 seconds
    c. 10 seconds
    d. 3 seconds

25. Unless they are refrigerated or stored in dry ice, heat-treated 2017-T rivets must be driven within what period after quenching?
    a. 1 minute
    b. 10 minutes
    c. 12 hours
    d. 1 hour

Chapter 4
Aircraft Riveting

MULTIPLE CHOICE
QUESTIONS

name:

date:

1. Describe the parts of a rivet. How does a rivet change during installation?

2. What do the marks on rivet heads indicate, generally? What do specific markings indicate?

ANALYSIS
QUESTIONS

name:

date:

3. What problems may arise if you use a rivet that is either too long or too short for the situation?

4. On a $1/4$ inch-diameter rivet, how wide should a properly headed bucktail be? How high should it be?

5. Describe the process of hand riveting.

6. In what sources can you find acceptability standards for rivet work? What is a good common-sense rule for testing whether a rivet is acceptable?

7. If you need to install a flush rivet on a curved surface, should you countersink it or dimple it? Why?

8. What would you take into consideration when inspecting a dimpled rivet installation?

9. Describe how you would go about drilling out a round-headed rivet.

10. What can you do if the rivet hole is just a little bit oversized?

1. A _____ removes the concentration of stress between the bolt head and shank, allowing an increase in bearing strength.

2. The ability of a fastener to bring two or more layers of material together is called _____ .

3. A rivet is made with a manufactured head, and another head, called a _____ is formed when the rivet is installed.

4. A rivet with a rounded head is called a _____ head rivet.

5. A rivet with a flat head is called a _____ rivet.

6. _____ fasteners can be used when an aircraft technician does not have the access required to form or install a locking head or a buckhead.

7. The diameter of a friction-lock rivet must be increased _____ when it replaces a solid-shank rivet.

8. The two styles of available CherryMAX® rivets are the bulbed and _____ .

9. When installing special straight-pin fasteners, exact _____ as recommended by the manufacturer, are necessary to produce the required strength.

10. The reason lockbolts and other special fasteners are not used extensively in general aviation is that the installation tools for them are very _____ .

11. The unthreaded portion of a bolt shank is called the _____ .

12. The hex-head bolt (AN3 through AN20) is an all-purpose _____ used for applications involving tension and shear loads where a light-drive fit is permissible.

13. A _____ may be self-locking or non-self-locking.

14. _____ , commonly called nut plates, are used in places where the installation of a normal nut is not possible, like inspection panels and access doors.

15. Instrument mounting-type _____ are used to hold flight instruments or engine instruments in an aircraft's instrument panel.

16. _____ are the most commonly used threaded fastening devices on aircraft.

17. The last number in a screw identification code, like AN501B-416-7, gives the length of the screw in _____ of an inch.

Chapter 5
Aircraft Hardware

FILL IN THE BLANK QUESTIONS

name:

date:

Chapter 5
Aircraft Hardware

18. _____ screws are made of alloyed steel, heat-treated, and can be used as structural bolts.

19. _____ pins are used in joints that carry shear loads and where the absence of play is essential.

20. The AN960 and AN970 _____ are used under hex nuts.

FILL IN THE BLANK
QUESTIONS

name:

date:

21. Heli-Coils or _____ sleeves can be used to repair or replace damaged internal threads.

22. A 7x7 flexible cable has seven _____ made up of seven wires.

23. _____ fittings are pressed onto a cable using a hand or power tool.

24. _____ is the process of securing bolts, nuts, screws, and other fasteners so that they do not work loose.

25. Safety wire must be applied so that the pull exerted by the wire will tend to _____ the bolt.

1. What type of aluminum rivet is not used for structural repair work?
   a. 1100
   b. 2117
   c. 2017
   d. 5056

2. For what purpose was aluminum alloy 5056 developed?
   a. Structural repairs involving monel
   b. Fastening aluminum sheet metal to longerons
   c. Attaching magnesium skins to the control surfaces of light aircraft
   d. Cold fusion of multiple sheets of metal

3. The standard angle of the metal between the shank and the head of a countersunk rivet is:
   a. 90°
   b. 100°
   c. 110°
   d. 120°

4. CherryMAX®, CherryLOCK®, Hi-Lok®, and Allfast® are types of:
   a. Friction-lock blind rivets
   b. Universal protruding head rivets
   c. Solid-shank rivets
   d. Mechanical-lock blind rivets

5. Which of these fasteners can be installed with an Allen wrench and a box wrench?
   a. Allfast®/Olympic-lok®
   b. Hi-Lok®
   c. Hi-Shear
   d. CherryMAX®

6. What type of fastener is used to obtain high strength in areas like landing gear, engine-to-wing spar attachments, and wing-to-fuselage joints?
   a. Lockbolts
   b. Hi-Lites
   c. Friction-lock blind rivets
   d. American National Coarse bolts

7. A disadvantage of a CherryBUCK® fastener is:
   a. Increase in foreign object damage (FOD) around jet engine intakes
   b. Cannot be used on included surfaces
   c. Inability to take up a multiple stack of sheet metal
   d. Requires expensive installation tools

8. Close-tolerance NAS bolts are marked with what on the head of the bolt?
   a. A triangle
   b. A square
   c. A dimple
   d. A distinctive color

9. American National Coarse, American Standard Unified Coarse, and American Standard Unified Fine are types of what?
   a. Thread series on aircraft bolts, screws, and nuts
   b. Alloys used in aircraft bolts, screws, and nuts
   c. Aircraft maintenance standards
   d. Head shapes used on aircraft bolts and screws

10. Which type of bolt is manufactured to receive wire for safetying?
    a. Clevis
    b. Drilled-head
    c. Standard hex
    d. Internal wrenching

Chapter 5
Aircraft Hardware

MULTIPLE CHOICE QUESTIONS

name:

date:

Chapter 5
Aircraft Hardware

MULTIPLE CHOICE
QUESTIONS

name:

date:

11. When replacing an internal-wrenching bolt, it is only acceptable to use:
    a. A standard AN hex bolt and washer, because they are just as strong
    b. A close-tolerance bolt, since these are machined to a high level of accuracy
    c. A clevis bolt, because it can handle both shear and tension loads
    d. Another internal-wrenching bolt, because of its strength

12. What kind of nut is assigned part number AN310?
    a. Plain
    b. Castle or castellated
    c. Castellated shear
    d. Self-locking

13. Which letter in nut part number AN310B5R indicates the material used to manufacture the nut?
    a. A
    b. B
    c. R
    d. N

14. What kind of nut is used on aircraft to provide tight connections that will not shake loose under severe vibration?
    a. Wing nut
    b. Castle
    c. Self-locking
    d. Plain

15. Fillister, flat, truss, and round are common types of:
    a. Screw heads
    b. Bolt heads
    c. Self-locking nuts
    d. Pins

16. Roll, flathead, cotter, and taper are common types of:
    a. Screw heads
    b. Bolt heads
    c. Self-locking nuts
    d. Pins

17. Under which of these conditions may lockwashers be used?
    a. With fasteners to primary or secondary structures
    b. Where they are exposed to the airflow
    c. Against soft material
    d. None of these

18. Dzus, Camloc, and Airloc are brand names of:
    a. Aircraft bolts
    b. Cowling fasteners
    c. Cables
    d. Replacement sleeves

19. Which of these is a disadvantage of a cable linkage system in aircraft?
    a. Can be rigged to eliminate backlash
    b. Tension must be adjusted frequently because of stretching and temperature changes
    c. Must be protected from corrosion
    d. Both b and c

20. A device used to make minor adjustments in cable length or to adjust cable tension is called a:
    a. Nicopress oval sleeve
    b. Fork-end swaged terminal
    c. Turnbuckle
    d. Camloc fastener

21. When using the double-twist method of safety wiring, small-diameter wire (0.020 inches) is most effective at how many twists per inch?
    a. 6
    b. 8
    c. 10
    d. 12

22. Safety wiring always terminates with a:
    a. Single twist
    b. Cotter pin
    c. Pigtail
    d. Self-locking nut

23. Which of these types of safetying is generally used with castellated nuts or drilled bolts?
    a. Cotter pin
    b. Turnbuckle
    c. Shock absorber cord
    d. Single twist

24. What type of gasket should not be used any place that it will come in contact with gasoline or oil?
    a. Cork
    b. Copper
    c. Rubber
    d. Asbestos

25. The two components of a two-part sealant are called:
    a. The base compound and the thinner
    b. The base compound and the accelerator
    c. The thinner and the accelerator
    d. The curer and the base compound

Chapter 5

Aircraft Hardware

MULTIPLE CHOICE QUESTIONS

name:

date:

1. What factors increase the strength of a joint created by using fasteners? What factor restricts the size of the fastener and the strength of the joint?

2. What physical changes take place when a solid rivet is driven?

3. What is the difference between friction-lock and mechanical-lock blind rivets?

4. Describe how you install a Hi-Lok rivet.

5. Describe the steel-alloy and aluminum-alloy bolts that can be used in primary aircraft structures. In what situations should you avoid using certain types of bolts?

Chapter 5
Aircraft Hardware

6. Where are self-locking nuts commonly used on aircraft?

ANALYSIS
QUESTIONS

name:

date:

7. What three types of screws are used on aircraft? Briefly describe the use of each type.

8. Describe four types of pins used in aircraft repair and their installation.

9. What is the most important feature of cowling fasteners?

10. Describe how you would safety an oil cap using the double-twist method.

1. _____ is the drawing of an engineering picture of an object.

2. Prints are _____ of the original engineering drawings.

3. _____ are used to show internal detail more clearly than is possible in other types of drawings.

4. A _____ view shows an object as if it had been cut in half.

5. A _____ represents mechanical, electrical, or electronic action without necessarily expressing the construction of an object or system of objects.

6. An _____ diagram shows only the external connections between units in an electrical system.

7. A _____ electrical wiring diagram shows sketches of the components and the connection between them, but generally does not indicate the location of equipment.

8. A drawing that shows several views of an object from different sides is called an _____ drawing.

9. In an _____ drawing, all lines that are parallel on the part being depicted are also parallel in the drawing, which shows a three-dimensional object approximately the way the eye would see it.

10. In technical drawings, fractions are always drawn with a _____ division line.

11. _____ is the acceptable variation from the specific dimension given on a drawing.

12. In dimensioning distances between holes in an object, the dimension is usually given in the distance between the _____ of the holes.

13. A drawing may include a _____ , which is a list of the parts and other items necessary for the fabrication or assembly of the component depicted in the drawing.

14. _____ on a drawing help to indicate the location of a particular part, much like the numbers and letters printed on the border of a map do.

15. _____ are used to identify a given point on an aircraft within one cubic inch.

16. _____ stations are measured in inches vertically from a datum that may be the ground, above the ground, or even below the ground.

FILL IN THE BLANK QUESTIONS

name:

date:

17. The letters RWS indicate a _____ , or a point a certain number of inches from the centerline of the aircraft.

18. To _____ a line or angle means to divide the line or angle into two equal parts.

19. When one variable is charted on the horizontal axis and the other is charted on the vertical axis, the graph is called _____ .

FILL IN THE BLANK
QUESTIONS

20. A 4-by-6-inch sheet of film that can hold thousands of pages of written information is called a _____ .

name:

date:

1. A drawing that supplies complete information for the construction of a single part is called:
    a. A detail drawing
    b. An installation drawing
    c. A logic flow chart
    d. An assembly drawing

2. A drawing that depicts the relationship between two or more parts is called:
    a. A detail drawing
    b. An installation drawing
    c. A logic flow chart
    d. An assembly drawing

3. Single-line, schematic, connection, and interconnect are types of what kind of drawing?
    a. Logic flow chart
    b. Exploded view
    c. Electrical wiring
    d. Orthographic projection

4. The main view in an orthographic projection drawing is usually the front view. If the view from the right side of the object is shown, to which side of the main view will it be?
    a. Left
    b. Above
    c. Below
    d. Right

5. This type of isometric drawing shows the oblique side of an object at a 30 or 45 degree angle and in $1/2$ scale.
    a. Oblique
    b. Cabinet
    c. Cavalier
    d. Perspective

6. What does a solid, thick line in an engineering drawing indicate?
    a. A hidden line
    b. Visible line or outline
    c. A center line
    d. A dimension line

7. What does a thin line made up of alternating long and short dashes in an engineering drawing indicate?
    a. A hidden line
    b. A visible line or outline
    c. A center line
    d. A dimension line

8. What does a medium line of short, evenly spaced dashes indicate in an engineering drawing?
    a. A dimension line
    b. A hidden line
    c. A cutting plane
    d. An outline

9. What does a leader line do in an engineering drawing?
    a. Shows the distance between the points of its two opposite arrowheads
    b. Indicate invisible edges
    c. Indicate the alternative position of parts or the relative position of a missing part
    d. Indicate a part or portion to which a note or other reference applies

10. A dimension that reads (in inches) 3.350 ± 0.004 means the acceptable size of the part is:
    a. 3.350 to 3.354 inches
    b. 3.346 to 3.354 inches
    c. 3.346 to 3.350 inches
    d. 3.348 to 3.352 inches

Chapter 6
Aircraft Drawings

MULTIPLE CHOICE
QUESTIONS

name:

date:

11. The name or number of a drawing, the scale to which it is drawn, the date, and the name of the firm and draftsperson can usually be found in what part of an engineering drawing?
    a. Upper left
    b. Title block
    c. Scale
    d. Standards

12. If the scale on a drawing says "1 inch equals 6 inches," a line on the drawing that is 2 inches long indicates a part on the object that is how many inches long?
    a. 2 inches
    b. 6 inches
    c. 8 inches
    d. 12 inches

13. If the scale on a drawing says, "2 inches equals 1 inch," a line in the drawing that is 3 inches long indicates a part on the drawing that is how long?
    a. 2 inches
    b. 1 inch
    c. 1 1/2 inches
    d. 6 inches

14. The changes to a drawing are listed in this part of a technical drawing:
    a. Bill of materials
    b. Revision block
    c. Zone numbers
    d. Standards

15. Which of these stations might indicate, in inches, the horizontal distance from the nose of an aircraft?
    a. Fuselage station
    b. Waterline station
    c. Buttock line station
    d. Wing station

16. What type of station is measured from the only datum that is the same on all aircraft?
    a. Fuselage station
    b. Waterline station
    c. Buttock line station
    d. Central station

17. A type of graph that shows the relation between three variables is:
    a. Diagraph
    b. Nomograph
    c. Rectilinear
    d. Circular

18. Which of these methods is used to reduce paperwork storage space for aircraft maintenance?
    a. Microfilm
    b. Microfiche
    c. Computer data storage
    d. All of these

19. Drawings or information stored on 35 mm film is said to be:
    a. Microfilmed
    b. Microfiched
    c. Digitized
    d. A hoped-for future result of research

20. The use of a computer to record maintenance, find repair procedures, order parts is called:
    a. Computer assisted design (CAD)
    b. Computer assisted management (CAM)
    c. Computer assisted maintenance (CAM)
    d. Microfiche maintenance and performance (MMP)

1. Describe the difference between artistic drawings and technical drawings.

2. What can sectional drawing show that other drawings cannot? What types of lines are used to clarify sectional drawings?

ANALYSIS
QUESTIONS

name:

date:

3. Describe three types of isometric drawings.

4. What is a perspective drawing? When is it used, and when is it not used?

5. How are dimensions shown in an engineering drawing?

6. Many parts on the left side of an aircraft have a corresponding part on the right side. An engineering drawing may show only one of these parts. Which one would it show, and how would the part for the other side be noted?

ANALYSIS
QUESTIONS

name:

7. Describe how you can find the center of a line using a pencil compass rather than a ruler.

date:

8. Describe how you can divide a line into an equal number of parts using a pencil compass and a ruler, but without measuring the line.

9. Why might an aircraft repair technician have to have or develop some sketching ability?

10. What sort of paper material tends to fill up an aircraft repair office, and how can it be reduced?

1. Of all the aircraft metals, pure _____ is the most easily formed.

2. Generally, the _____ the metal, the sharper it can be bent.

3. The radius of bend of a sheet of metal is the radius of the bend as measured on the _____of the curve.

4. According to Table 7-2-1, the standard minimum radius for a annealed aluminum alloy 0.064 inches thick is _____ of an inch.

5. The _____ is the length of material required for the bend.

6. Bending metal compresses the material on the inside of the curve and stretches the material on the outside of it, but between these areas, there is a _____ not affected by either force.

7. An _____ formula is one that was derived solely by experiment and observation without reference to scientific principles.

8. In most shops, _____ tables are available in order to save time and avoid tricky calculations.

9. The _____ is the point of intersection of the lines extending from the outside surfaces of the metal on either side of a bend.

10. The _____ are the starting and end points of a bend.

11. To find the set-back for angles other than 90 degrees, you have to use a set-back table, also known as a _____ , to find one component of the formula.

12. Find the _____ line by measuring out one radius from the bend tangent line that will be inserted against the radius form block.

13. To create a _____ for the nose piece of a sheet metal brake, place a wide strip of annealed aluminum in the brake, adjust the brake for its thickness, and bend the piece to its maximum degree of bend.

14. Holes drilled at the intersection of two bends to make room for the material in the flanges are called _____ .

15. Angles can be curved by stretching or shrinking either flange. _____ one of the flanges is usually preferred, since it is more easily accomplished.

16. You should flatten a _____ starting at the apex (or closed end) and working toward the edge of the flange.

Chapter 7

Forming Processes

FILL IN THE BLANK QUESTIONS

name:

date:

Chapter 7
Forming Processes

FILL IN THE BLANK
QUESTIONS

name:

date:

17. The flanges on curved parts are formed over specially-made _____ blocks.

18. When you _____ a piece of metal, you finish a formed piece and remove small irregularities with a specialized hammer and a stake.

19. A bumping die should be at least _____ larger in all dimensions than the form requires.

20. A _____ is an offset formed on an angle strip to provide clearance for a sheet or an extrusion.

21. Holes cut in rib sections, fuselage frames, or other structural parts to decrease weight are called _____ .

22. When drilling holes in stainless steel, the speed of the drill should be about _____ the speed required to drill mild steel.

23. When it is necessary to drill several deep holes in stainless steel, apply a _____ to the material immediately upon starting the drill to avoid overheating.

24. Wing and empennage leading edges are commonly produced on a _____ .

25. Buckets, tubs, pans, and some funnels can be formed on a _____ .

1. When marking layouts on aluminum or aluminum alloys, use:
   a. A lead pencil
   b. A metal scriber
   c. A soft wax-charcoal pencil
   d. A permanent marker

2. The sharpest bend that can be placed in the metal without critically weakening the part is called:
   a. The minimum radius of bend
   b. The maximum radius of bend
   c. The set-back
   d. The brake or sight line

MULTIPLE CHOICE QUESTIONS

name:

date:

3. The neutral line list located approximately how far from the inside of the bend?
   a. Half the thickness of the metal
   b. 0.445 times the length of the bend radius
   c. 0.445 times the thickness of the metal
   d. $2\pi(R + 1/2T)/4$

4. The formula for calculating the bend allowance for a 90-degree bend is:
   a. $2\pi(R + 1/2T)/4$
   b. $2\pi(R + 1/2T)$
   c. $(0.01743R)+(0.0078T) \times N$
   d. $2\pi(RT)+(0.0078T)/4$

5. The formula for calculating the bend allowance for a bend of any angle is:
   a. $2\pi(RT)+(0.0078T)/4$
   b. $(1.01743R)+(0.78T) \times N$
   c. $2\pi(R + 1/2T)/4$
   d. $(0.01743R)+(0.0078T) \times N$

6. To calculate the set-back for a 90-degree bend, you add:
   a. The inside radius of the bend to the thickness of the sheet
   b. The length of the bend tangent lines to the thickness of the sheet
   c. The bend allowance to the inside radius
   d. The inside radius of the bend to twice the thickness of the sheet

7. If a bend is made with the sight line located too far from the clamp:
   a. The part will be too short
   b. The part will be just right—you have to allow for a set-back from the line
   c. The part will be to long
   d. The brake will jam or otherwise not function properly

8. To form a 90-degree, 1-inch flange in a piece of metal that is 0.040 inches thick, how far from the edge would you mark the bend tangent line? (The radius of the bend will be 1/4 inch.)
   a. 0.71 inches
   b. 1 inch
   c. 0.67 inches
   d. 0.75 inches

9. The diameter of a relief hole varies with the thickness of the metal, but in aluminum alloy stock between 0.072 and 0.128 inches thick, they should not be less than:
   a. 1/8 inch
   b. 1/4 inch
   c. 3/16 inch
   d. 5/16 inch

10. Stretching metal in hand forming to make it balloon is called:
    a. Joggling
    b. Bumping
    c. Laying out
    d. Springing back

Chapter 7
Forming Processes

MULTIPLE CHOICE
QUESTIONS

name:

date:

11. If you drive material you are hand forming slightly further than the actual bend requires, you are allowing for:
   a. Spring back
   b. Fall back
   c. Common irregularities
   d. Form block rounding

12. To curve an angle strip by shrinking one of the flanges and using a V-block, you lay the piece with:
   a. One of the flanges inserted into the groove of the V-block
   b. With one of the flanges flat perpendicular to the V in the block and the other flange pointing upward
   c. Parallel to the V in the block
   d. Any way that feels comfortable

13. If the curve of a flange must be relatively sharp, you will use these tools:
   a. V-block and mallet
   b. Crimping pliers and shrinking block
   c. Cornice brake and nose shim
   d. Form block, V-block, and ball bearings

14. Which of these parts is often is a curved part with both inside (concave) and outside (convex) flanges?
   a. Streamlined cover plate
   b. Nose rib
   c. Wing fillet
   d. Most control surfaces

15. Which of these parts is often formed using block or die bumping?
   a. Streamlined cover plate
   b. Nose rib
   c. Wing fillet
   d. Most control surfaces

16. Which of these parts is often formed using bumping on a sandbag?
   a. Streamlined cover plate
   b. Landing gear
   c. Wing fillet
   d. Most control surfaces

17. When bumping metal into a blister, you should always start at what part of the form?
   a. The middle
   b. The side to your right
   c. The side to your left
   d. The edges

18. Bumping metal with the use of a sandbag can be challenging because:
   a. The sandbag is harder than the metal
   b. The sandbag indentation will shift as you work the metal and must be rechecked periodically
   c. The metal must be cut to exact size before proceeding
   d. You are not allowed to use a template

19. The depth of a joggle is based on:
   a. The length of the piece
   b. The width of the piece
   c. The thickness of the material to be cleared
   d. The metallic composition of the piece you are working on

20. The purpose of flanges around lightening holes is:
   a. To strengthen the area around which material has been removed
   b. To further lighten the piece
   c. To ensure a smooth fit with another structural piece
   d. Increase aerodynamic properties

1. What affect does temper condition have on forming operations for various metals and alloys?

2. What precautions or steps should you take when forming metal to avoid marring the metal surface?

ANALYSIS
QUESTIONS

name:

date:

3. Calculate the bend allowance for a 90-degree bend in a sheet of aluminum alloy 0.072 inches thick, when the radius of the bend is 1/2 inch.

4. Find the bend allowance for a 100-degree bend in a sheet of aluminum 0.032 inches thick, when the radius of the bend is 1/4 of an inch. Use the bend allowance table, Table 7-2-2A and Table 7-2-2B.

5. Figure the set-back allowance for a 120-degree bend with a radius of 3/8 of an inch in an aluminum sheet 0.064 inches thick.

Chapter 7
Forming Processes

6. You must lay out a flat channel with two 90-degree flanges. One flange will be 3/4 inch high, the base will be 2 inches wide, and the other flange will be 2.5 inches high. The metal is 0.081 inches thick, and the radius of each bend is 1/4 inch. Describe your calculations. What is the total width of the material?

ANALYSIS
QUESTIONS

name:

date:

7. Describe how you could duplicate a part to create a template using a straight edge, pencil compass, and French curve.

8. Under what circumstances could you form a straight-line bend by hand instead of with the use of a cornice brake or bar folder? What procedures would you follow?

9. Describe how to form a flanged angle by shrinking part of the metal using hand tools. Which direction would the flange ultimately be pointing if you were to create it by shrinking?

10. How would you form a wood block into a female die used to create a blister?

1. Since information on the design loads at work in various structural parts of an airplane are seldom available to the field repair technician, the problem of repairing a damaged section is usually solved by an attempt to _____ the original part.

2. When the aircraft structural repair manual does not exist, refer to _____ or other approved information.

3. Tension is a force that tends to _____ a structural member.

4. Compression is a force that tends to _____ a structural member.

5. Torsion is the force that tends to _____ a structural member.

6. In order to reduce the possibility of cracks starting from the corners of a cutout, try to make cutouts either _____ or oval.

7. To determine the number of rivets to be used on each side of a repair, multiply the length of the break by the thickness of the original material by _____ and then divide by either the shearing or bearing strength of the rivets, whichever is smaller.

8. Maintaining the original contour of the piece being repaired is especially important on _____.

9. Unless otherwise directed, treat all contacting surfaces in the area of a repair for resistance to _____ regardless of the composition of the metal.

10. When removing the damaged portion of the piece you are repairing, trim away enough material to include all _____ that extend out from the damage.

11. In repairing smooth skin, the size and shape of the patch are determined, in general, by the number of _____ required in the repair.

12. A _____ is the part of a panel between adjacent stringers and bulkheads.

13. New _____ are permissible only when existing openings do not permit access to a damaged area.

14. An access door consists of a supporting or reinforcing ring and a _____ .

15. In a leading edge repair that goes from cap strip to cap strip, the material for the splice plates must be _____ heavier than the original skin.

16. In standard _____ corrugation, the inside radius of a crest fits into the outside radius of a valley, making it possible to overlap sections.

FILL IN THE BLANK QUESTIONS

name:

date:

17. If not more than _____ of the cross-sectional area of a bulkhead must be removed, use a patch plate and filler plate.

18. In a longeron repair, in order to reduce the number of large-diameter 2024-T rivets, you may substitute _____ .

19. When making a truss tubing repair, take the _____ of the tube as the length of the damage.

20. The trailing edge is considered a _____ area of the aircraft, so repairs only need to restore the member to its original shape and rigidity.

21. Repairs to a _____ web must restore the original strength of the member.

22. The methods and procedures you use in all repairs are determined by a process called

_____ .

23. Small general aviation aircraft typically do not have a structural repair manual, but defer to the FAA's _____ for day-to-day repair procedures.

24. At a _____ , primary responsibility for maintenance records lies with the head inspector.

25. If an aircraft part is not obtained from the aircraft manufacturer or one of its agents, from the holder of an STC, or someone who has a PMA, they are _____ .

1. When an airplane is on the ground, forces on the wings, fuselage, and empennage point:
   a. Upward
   b. Downward
   c. Laterally
   d. None of these; there are no forces acting on a grounded airplane

2. Which of these is considered a basic stress on an aircraft?
   a. Compression
   b. Bending
   c. Twisting
   d. Torsion

3. Which of these is considered a combination stress on an aircraft?
   a. Compression
   b. Torsion
   c. Tension
   d. Shear

4. A force that acts in such a way as to slide adjacent parts of material past each other is:
   a. Tension
   b. Compression
   c. Shear
   d. Bending

5. A force that results from a combination of tension and compression acting in opposite directions is:
   a. Dynamic compression
   b. Torsion
   c. Tension
   d. Bending

6. Material used in replacement or reinforcements should never be:
   a. Stronger material than the original, but of a lighter gauge
   b. Weaker material than the original, but of a heavier gauge
   c. Identical to the original material
   d. None of these

7. To determine the size of rivets to be used for a repair, you can:
   a. Use the size used by the manufacturer in the next parallel row inboard or forward on the fuselage
   b. Multiply the thickness of the thickest skin by three, then use the next-largest size rivets
   c. Either a or b
   d. Neither a nor b is acceptable

8. Small dents, scratches, cracks, or holes that can be sanded or hammered out or repaired without the use of additional material are classified as:
   a. Negligible damage
   b. Repairable damage
   c. Damage necessitating replacement
   d. Corrosion damage

9. Damage so severe that the part cannot be restored to its original strength is classified as:
   a. Negligible damage
   b. Repairable damage
   c. Damage necessitating replacement
   d. Corrosion damage

10. The regular amount of outer edge material included in a patch is:
    a. $2\,1/2$ rivet diameters
    b. 3 rivet diameters
    c. 4 rivet diameters
    d. $4\,1/2$ rivet diameters

Chapter 8
Structural Repair

MULTIPLE CHOICE QUESTIONS

name:

date:

Chapter 8
Structural Repair

MULTIPLE CHOICE QUESTIONS

name:

date:

11. Panel section damage that, after being trimmed, has less than 8 1/2 manufacturer's rivet diameters of material left inside the members requires a patch:
    a. Fastened by only one row of rivets along the panel edge
    b. That extends over the members plus an extra row of rivets outside the members
    c. As wide as the distance between the members, plus an extra row of rivets inside the members
    d. Identical in size to the removed material, with rivets matching the manufacturer's pattern

12. Installation of an access door must be approved by:
    a. The aircraft owner
    b. The FAA designated engineering representative (DER)
    c. Your supervisor
    d. The FAA field engineering supervisor (FES)

13. The material used as a filler plate in a longeron repair must be:
    a. Thinner than the original material
    b. Thicker than the original material
    c. The same thickness as the original material
    d. None of these; the tensile strength of the material is more important than the thickness

14. In determining the length of the break in an extruded T cap strip repair of a spar, use:
    a. The width of the base of the T plus the length of the leg
    b. One-half the width of the base of the T plus the length of the leg
    c. The width of the base of the T plus the length of the spar
    d. The width of the base of the T plus the length of the splice plate

15. This manual is sometimes called "the bible of aircraft repair."
    a. The Manufacturer's Repair Manual
    b. AC43.13-1B
    c. FAA Form 337
    d. ATA Specification 100

16. The various transport aircraft manufacturers publish repair manuals the follow the outline of:
    a. The Manufacturer's Repair Manual
    b. AC43.13-1B
    c. FAA Form 337
    d. ATA Specification 100

17. A document created as part of the design and approval process and that contains all the standards to which the aircraft was design as well as all original and optional equipment in the design is called a:
    a. Designated engineering representation
    b. Type certificate
    c. AC43.13-1B
    d. Certified repair record

18. Approved changes and improvements to an original design, which can be in the form of approval documents or kits that include specially fabricated parts and assemblies, are called:
    a. Type certificates
    b. Supplemental type certificates
    c. Auxiliary type certificates
    d. Enhanced type certificates

19. An FAA Advisory Circular that applies to maintenance and repair records is:
    a. AC43.19E, "Instructions for Completion of FAA Form 337, Major Repairs and Alterations"
    b. AC43-9B, "Maintenance Records"
    c. AC20-109A, "Service Difficulty Program (General Aviation)"
    d. All of these

20. A document that can help you recognize unapproved parts used in aircraft maintenance is:
    a. AC43.19E, "Instructions for Completion of FAA Form 337, Major Repairs and Alterations"
    b. AC21-109A, "Detecting and Reporting Suspected Unapproved Parts"
    c. AC1040-E, "You Know You Have an Unapproved Part When…"
    d. AC21-109D, "On the Detection, Removal, and Reporting of Unapproved Parts"

1. Describe the forces that act on the parts of an aircraft on the ground. How do forces change when the aircraft is in flight?

ANALYSIS
QUESTIONS

name:

date:

2. What two basic stresses act together to form bending stress? How does one basic stress act to form torsion?

3. What factors should you consider when assessing a structural damage repair and in making an estimate of the work and materials required?

4. Calculate the number of 2024-T rivets required to repair a 3-inch break in material 0.064 inches thick?

5. When is a rivet under double shear?

6. Say a hard landing overloads one of the landing gear and causes it to be sprung. What should you take into account when assessing the damage?

7. Why is it best to use an elongated octagonal patch for a smooth skin repair?

8. You are repairing the leading edge of a wing. The wing material is 0.040 inches thick, you must use 2117-T rivets, and the distance from cap strip to cap strip is 12 inches. How many rivets will you need? Remember, you must use a splice plate at both ends of the patch.

9. If about two-thirds of a former's cross-sectional area is damaged, how should you repair it?

10. What is similar between the manuals for various models of transport aircraft, if the manuals are based on ATA Specification 100? Why was ATA Specification 100 implemented?

1. Corrosion is a natural phenomenon in which chemical or electrochemical action converts metal into a metallic _____ such as oxide, hydroxide, or sulfate.

2. Corrosion can take place _____ as well as on the surface.

3. A visible dye-penetrant test consists of dye penetrant, dye remover-emulsifier, and _____ .

4. There are two basic _____ systems for corrosion inspection: pulsed and resonance.

5. If the frequency of an ultrasonic wave is such at its wavelength is twice the thickness of a specimen, the _____ will arrive back at the transducer in the same phase as the original transmission.

6. An ultrasonic resonance system can be used to test the _____ of steel, cast iron, brass, nickel, and other metals.

7. _____ inspection techniques are used to located defects or flaws in airframe structures or engines with little or no disassembly.

8. The three major steps in the X-ray process are exposure to radiation, _____and interpretation of the radiograph.

9. The two main flaws that are visible in a radiograph are voids and _____ .

10. Prior to working with radiation hazard equipment, you must be familiar with—and apply—all the applicable Occupational Safety and Health Administration (OSHA) and _____ standards.

11. Dry corrosion is also known as _____ . It occurs when a metal is exposed to a gas containing oxygen.

12. Reactive compounds from exhaust gases or fumes from storage batteries frequently cause uniform _____ .

13. _____ corrosion is confined to small areas of the metal surface, while the remainder of the surface is unaffected.

14. Intergranular corrosion first consumes the material between the _____ and then attacks the grains themselves.

15. _____ is a severe form of intergranular corrosion characterized by the actual leafing out of corroded sections of metal away from the rest of the part.

16. The _____ in alloys provide a basis for galvanic action within the galvanic cells themselves.

FILL IN THE BLANK
QUESTIONS

name:

date:

17. Stress corrosion is the result of the combined effect of _____ and a corrosive environment.

18. Substances that are capable of causing or promoting a corrosive reaction are sometimes called corrosive _____ .

19. _____ live in jet fuels that are contaminated with water and iron oxides or mineral salts.

20. Relatively little corrosion trouble is to be expected with _____ if the original surface finish and insulation are adequately maintained.

21. _____ are prime spots for corrosion due to the dissimilar metal contact between the steel pins and the aluminum hinge.

22. In welded areas, corrosion may be caused by flux residues, which are _____ , meaning that they are capable of retaining moisture.

23. In cleaning an aluminum alloy surface in preparation for the removal of corrosion, it is important not to remove unnecessary amounts of the _____ , or the relatively pure aluminum, that is laminated to the alloy for corrosion protection.

24. Do not use _____ cleaners on stainless steels.

25. _____ is the most chemically active of the metals used in aircraft construction, and therefore the most difficult to protect from corrosion.

26. Spilled _____ is removed by using sodium bicarbonate (baking soda) or sodium borate (borax) 20 percent by weight dissolved in water.

27. In _____ , aluminum alloys are placed in an electrolytic bath, causing a thin film of aluminum to form on the surface.

28. In _____ , steels are coated with another metal in an electrolytic bath.

29. Dichromate treatment consists of boiling _____ in a solution of sodium dichromate.

30. A contact point between a magnesium alloy and nickel, for example, would require a _____ to prevent corrosion caused by dissimilar metals.

1. What is the most visible sign of corrosive attack?
   a. Corrosion deposits
   b. Dye-penetration indication
   c. Dirt
   d. Reading from a pulse-echo detection unit

2. What is the main disadvantage of a dye-penetrant inspection for corrosion?
   a. Doesn't work on aluminum
   b. Doesn't show a lack of bond between joined metals
   c. Messy and difficult to perform
   d. Doesn't show defects that are not open to the surface

MULTIPLE CHOICE
QUESTIONS

name:

date:

3. In pulsed ultrasonic testing, results of the scan appear:
   a. On a computer printout
   b. On a cathode-ray tube (CRT)
   c. On a straight beam
   d. Under an ultraviolet light

4. In straight-beam testing:
   a. Ultrasonic pulses are sent into the material at an acute angle
   b. Ultrasonic pulses are sent into the material and reflect back to the transducer from the opposite surface of the material
   c. Ultrasonic pulses reflect back to the transducer from another transducer located on the other side of the piece
   d. There are no ultrasonic pulses, but X-rays are used

5. Ultrasonic angle-beam testing can find:
   a. Discontinuities in areas that cannot be reached with standard straight-beam testing
   b. Some internal defects in plate and sheet stock
   c. Flaws whose parts lie at an angle to the plane of the part
   d. All of these

6. In what type of ultrasonic testing is the frequency continuously varied?
   a. Straight-beam
   b. Resonance
   c. Angle-beam
   d. Radiological

7. Radiological inspection of material uses what type of rays?
   a. X-rays
   b. Gamma rays
   c. Proton rays
   d. Either a or b, but never c

8. An important difference between oxidation of aluminum and oxidation of iron is:
   a. The film of aluminum oxide is porous and the metal will continue to react with the air even after it forms
   b. The film of aluminum oxide is unbroken and the reaction between the air and metal almost stops after the film is formed
   c. The film of iron oxide is unbroken and the reaction between the air and metal greatly slows after the film is formed
   d. The film of iron oxide prevents further corrosion because of a physical property called osmosis

9. Surface corrosion appears as a general roughening, etching, or pitting of the surface of a metal, frequently accompanied by:
   a. Wetness
   b. Massive pitting
   c. A powdery deposit
   d. Galvanic action

Chapter 9
Corrosion Control

MULTIPLE CHOICE
QUESTIONS

name:

date:

10. All forms of pitting have one thing in common:
    a. Deep penetration of the metal and damage out of proportion to the amount of metal consumed
    b. They occur between grain boundaries
    c. They are not visible to the naked eye
    d. The metal is marred over a wide area of its surface

11. Which of these metals is particularly susceptible to intergranular corrosion?
    a. Aluminum alloys
    b. Some stainless steels
    c. Iron
    d. Both a and b

12. Exfoliation corrosion is most often found on:
    a. Aircraft skin
    b. Extruded parts
    c. Longerons
    d. Heat-treated parts

13. Condensation from a salt-air atmosphere can serve as a:
    a. Exfoliant promoting intergranular corrosion
    b. Dissimilar metal promoting galvanic cell corrosion
    c. Electrolytic medium promoting galvanic cell corrosion
    d. A Group IV catalyst for intergranular corrosion

14. A highly damaging form of corrosion that occurs when two mating surfaces are subject to slight relative motion is called:
    a. Stress corrosion
    b. Fretting corrosion
    c. Filiform corrosion
    d. Oxygen cell corrosion

15. Metals coated with organic coatings are subject to which type of corrosion?
    a. Stress corrosion
    b. Fretting corrosion
    c. Filiform corrosion
    d. Oxygen cell corrosion

16. Washing soda, potash, and lime are examples of what kind of corrosive agent?
    a. Acids
    b. Alkalis
    c. Salts
    d. Micro-organisms

17. What kind of corrosive agent can completely penetrate sheet metal in as little as 3 minutes?
    a. Acid
    b. Water
    c. Salts
    d. Mercury

18. The most common contaminant in the air in industrial atmospheres is:
    a. Mercury
    b. Sulfur compounds
    c. Chlorides
    d. Fermium-108

19. Which of these can be used to control microorganisms in jet fuel tanks?
    a. Biocide treatment
    b. Slime treatment
    c. Water and iron oxide
    d. Ferrous alloys

20. Gaps, seams, hinges, fairings, and the areas around rivet heads, if they are in certain locations on the aircraft, are highly susceptible to corrosion caused by what?
    a. Battery fluid
    b. Engine exhaust
    c. Organic growth
    d. Fretting

21. When inspecting the wheel well and landing gear for corrosion, pay special attention to:
    a. Magnesium wheels
    b. Exposed rigid tubing
    c. Exposed position indicator switches and other electrical equipment
    d. All of these

22. You can treat superficial aluminum alloy corrosion with:
    a. A 10 percent solution of chromic acid and sulfuric acid
    b. Water-rinsable paint stripper
    c. A 5 percent solution of chromic acid
    d. Steel wool brushes

23. The most practical means of controlling the corrosion of steel is the complete removal of corrosion products by:
    a. Electronic means and then restoring corrosion-preventive coatings
    b. Mechanical means and then restoring corrosion-preventive coatings
    c. Applying phosphoric acid and then restoring corrosion-preventive coatings
    d. None of these

24. A treatment that deposits a layer of tin, as a protective paint base, on magnesium parts containing inserts or fasteners of a dissimilar metal is called:
    a. Phosphate rust-proofing
    b. Dichromate treatment
    c. Stannate immersion treatment
    d. Galvanic anodizing treatment

25. Zinc chromate primer, enamels, and chlorinated rubber compounds are examples of what type of coating commonly used to protect metals?
    a. Organic coating
    b. Cladding
    c. Plating
    d. Chrome-pickle coating

Chapter 9
Corrosion Control

MULTIPLE CHOICE QUESTIONS

name:

date:

1. How does the appearance of corrosion differ depending on the type of metal involved?

2. Describe the steps in testing for corrosion using a dye-penetrant process. If you use a visible penetrant-type developer, how will corrosion be indicated?

ANALYSIS
QUESTIONS

name:

date:

3. What are the differences between a pulsed and resonance ultrasonic system?

4. Describe what happens when a metal is oxidized.

5. Table 9-4-1 groups metals according to their rate of activity and ease with which they corrode. Which group of metals is the most active? List three metals that require the most protection from corrosion and three metals that require the least.

Chapter 9
Corrosion Control

6. Not all water is equally corrosive. Describe the factors that make certain types of water more corrosive. Where do you find the most corrosive water?

7. Why are deck areas behind lavatories, sinks, or ranges problem areas for corrosion?

8. What precautions should you take to avoid damaging anodized surfaces during corrosion removal?

9. Describe the steps you would take to remove corrosion from steel parts. (Assume the steel is not treated to a high level of hardness.)

10. How to you protect a dissimilar metal contact where magnesium is not one of the metals involved? What if magnesium is one of the metals?

1. _____ is the federal program that oversees basic workplace safety for all occupations.

2. Every commercial product used in aircraft maintenance is required by law to have a _____ that rates safety considerations.

3. A "3" in the red square of an MSDS indicates that the material is a serious _____ hazard.

FILL IN THE BLANK QUESTIONS

name:

4. The system where each cord and switch in a shop is padlocked is known as a _____ program.

5. Painted lines on the floor of a hangar are a safety measure used to keep _____ out of work areas.

date:

6. Two psychological factors that can affect safety when working around electricity are _____ and _____ .

7. Air hoses should be inspected frequently for _____ and _____ .

8. The first rule for safety around drill presses, lathes, milling machines, and grinders is to wear _____ .

9. You should always _____ a drill press or lathe before adjusting or measuring the work.

10. Do not stand in the _____ of a grinding wheel while operating it.

11. Fire requires fuel, heat, and _____ .

12. _____ extinguishers are recommended for Class A fires, but not for other types of fires.

13. Never use a CO_2 extinguisher on a _____ fire.

14. Halogenated hydrocarbon extinguishers are most effective on Class B and _____ fires.

15. Any old fire extinguishers containing the halogenated hydrocarbon _____ should be disposed of in accordance with EPA regulations, as it is not approved for fire fighting use.

FILL IN THE BLANK
QUESTIONS

name:

date:

16. Dry powder extinguishers are the best type to use on _____ fires, but are not recommended for use on aircraft because the chemical residue and dust left behind is difficult to clean up and can damage electronic equipment.

17. _____ is damage caused by any loose object to aircraft, people, or equipment.

18. Aircraft should be tied down headed _____ as nearly as possible depending on the location of the fixed tiedown points.

19. Tie ropes should never be tied to a _____ , as this practice can bend the part if the rope slips to a point where it has no slack.

20. _____ should remain inside an aircraft that is being jacked or hoisted.

1. The blue area in a Material Safety Data Sheet indicates:
   a. Flammable hazards
   b. Stability hazards
   c. Handling information
   d. General health hazards

2. The red area in a Material Safety Data Sheet indicates:
   a. Flammable hazards
   b. Stability hazards
   c. Handling information
   d. General health hazards

3. The yellow area in a Material Safety Data Sheet indicates:
   a. Flammable hazards
   b. Stability hazards
   c. Handling information
   d. General health hazards

4. The white area in a Material Safety Data Sheet indicates:
   a. Flammable hazards
   b. Stability hazards
   c. Handling information
   d. General health hazards

5. The single most important factor in preventing electrical fires is:
   a. Keeping the area around electrical work clean, uncluttered, and free of flammable substances
   b. Tagged circuit boxes
   c. The use of safety equipment such as gloves and face shields
   d. None of these apply to preventing electrical fires

6. To prevent injury when inflating any type of aircraft tires:
   a. Only fill tires when they have been removed from the aircraft
   b. Use tire cage guards
   c. Avoid over-inflating high-pressure tires
   d. Both b and c

7. At least how far away from a welding operation should aircraft be (assuming the welding is not being done on the aircraft itself)?
   a. 10 feet
   b. 35 feet
   c. 75 feet
   d. 100 feet

8. A fire in wood, cloth, paper, or upholstery, for example, is considered a:
   a. Class A fire
   b. Class B fire
   c. Class C fire
   d. Class D fire

9. A fire in flammable metal like magnesium is considered a:
   a. Class A fire
   b. Class B fire
   c. Class C fire
   d. Class D fire

10. Which of the following indicates the least toxicity in the Underwriters Laboratory (UL) classification system?
    a. 2
    b. 4
    c. 5
    d. 6

Chapter 10
Shop
Safety

MULTIPLE CHOICE
QUESTIONS

name:

date:

Chapter 10
Shop Safety

MULTIPLE CHOICE
QUESTIONS

name:

date:

11. Which of the following halogenated hydrocarbon fire extinguishers is recommended for aircraft use?
    a. Methyl bromide (Halon 1001)
    b. Bromochlorodifluoromethane (Halon 1211)
    c. Dibromodifluoromethane (Halon 1202)
    d. Both b and c

12. You should never approach a single-rotor helicopter from the rear when it is operating because:
    a. The pilot cannot see you
    b. The tail rotor is invisible when rotating
    c. It is impossible to gauge the height of the rotator blades
    d. Both a and b

13. Seaplanes have been saved from high-wind damage when they are tied down on land by this trick:
    a. Use of bowline knots
    b. Flooding the engine compartment
    c. Filling the floats with water
    d. Using the anchor that would have been used in mooring as an additional, unsecured tie loop

14. Ski planes can be tied down on ice or snow by attaching the tie lines to a:
    a. Deadman
    b. Chunk of ice
    c. Tiedown loop
    d. Control surface batten

15. If high winds are anticipated and a helicopter has to be parked in the open, you should tie down the helicopter itself as well as the:
    a. Wheel chocks
    b. Main rotor blades
    c. Tip socks
    d. Rotor brakes

1. What philosophies or general rules underlie the running of a safe shop?

2. What are some rules to follow when working with or around compressed gases?

ANALYSIS
QUESTIONS

name:

date:

3. If you have to do some welding on an aircraft, what precautions must you take?

4. What are some sources of noise on the flightline? What are some tools that require hearing protection when you are using them?

5. How can a jet engine by harmed by a foreign object? What other damage could this situation cause?